Betty N. Barlow

EASIEST VIOLIN DUETS FOR CHRISTMAS

BOOK ONE

CONTENTS

G. SCHIRMER, Inc.

DISTRIBUTED BY
HAL•LEONARD®
CORPORATION
7777 W. BLUEMOUND RD. P.O. BOX 13819 MILWAUKEE, WI 53213

EASIEST VIOLIN DUETS FOR CHRISTMAS
with Piano Accompaniment

Arrangements by
Betty M. Barlow

JOLLY OLD SAINT NICHOLAS

Traditional

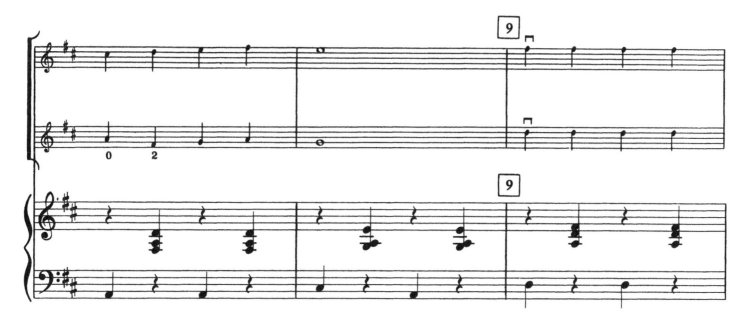

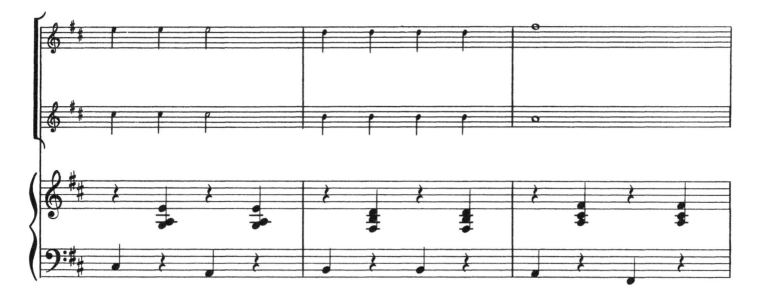

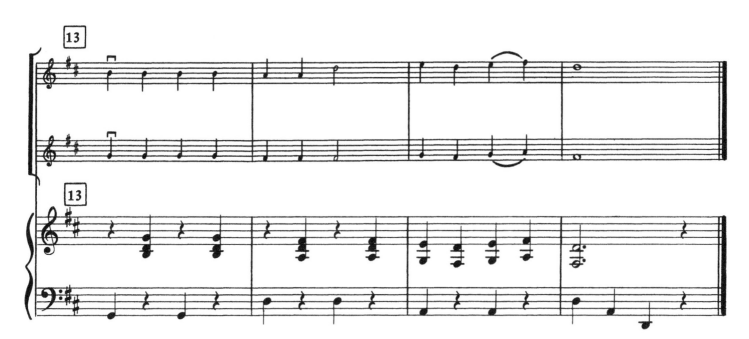

GOOD KING WENCESLAS

Traditional

1st Violin

2nd Violin

Piano

WE THREE KINGS OF ORIENT ARE

John H. Hopkins

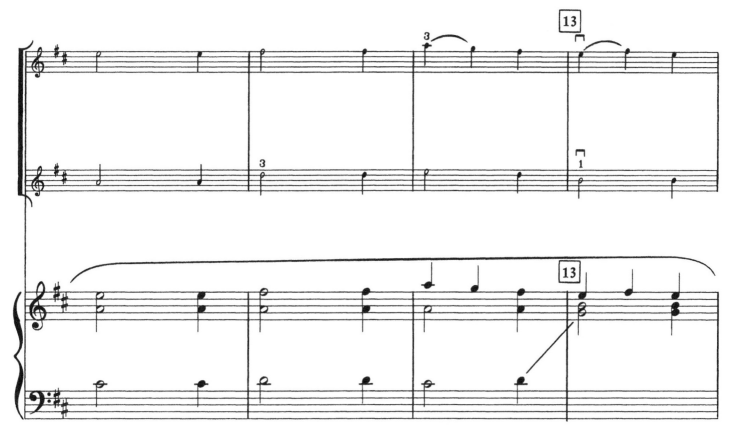

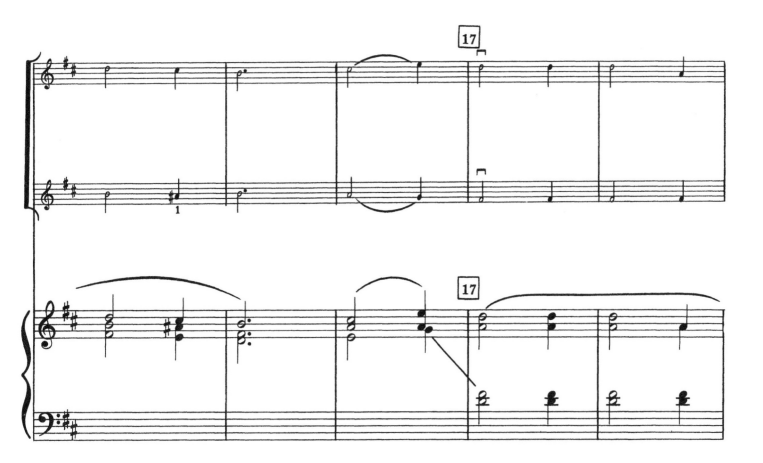

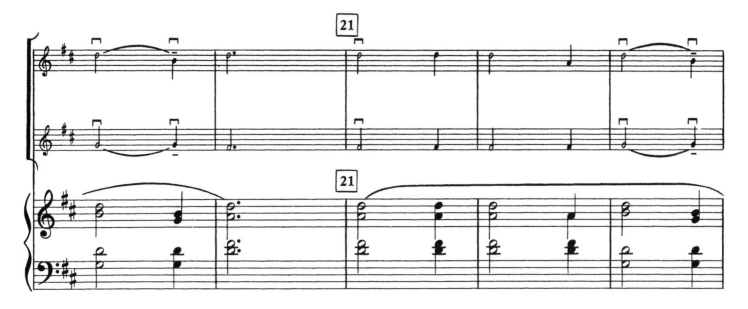

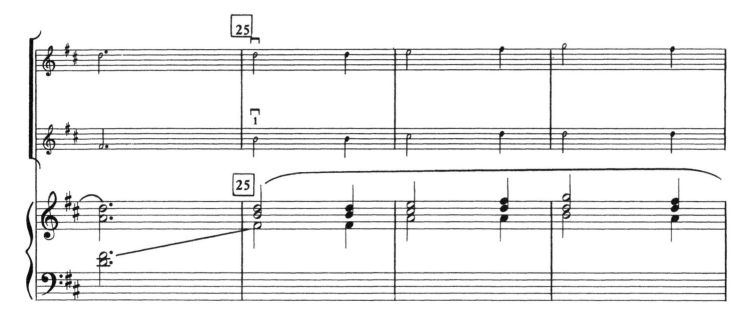

MARY HAD A BABY

Traditional

BRING A TORCH, JEANNETTE, ISABELLA

French Carol

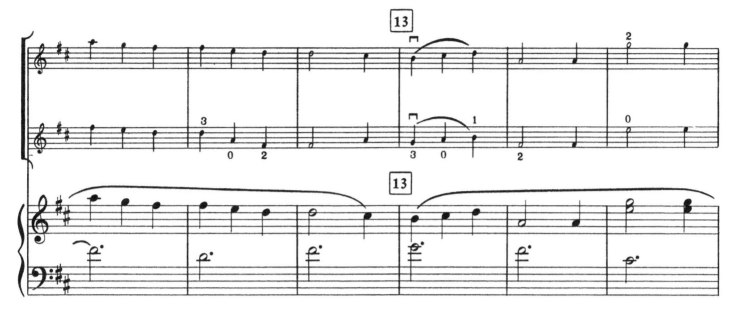

O COME LITTLE CHILDREN

J.A.P. Schulz

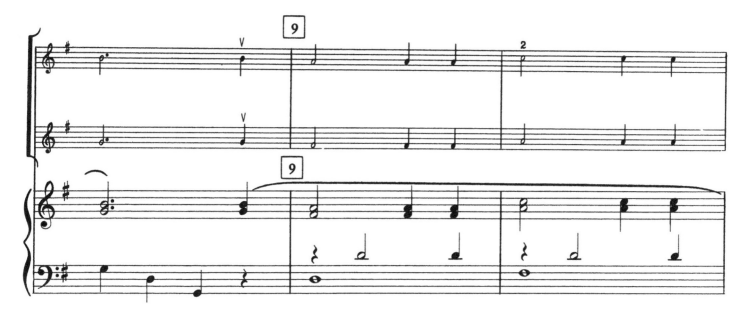

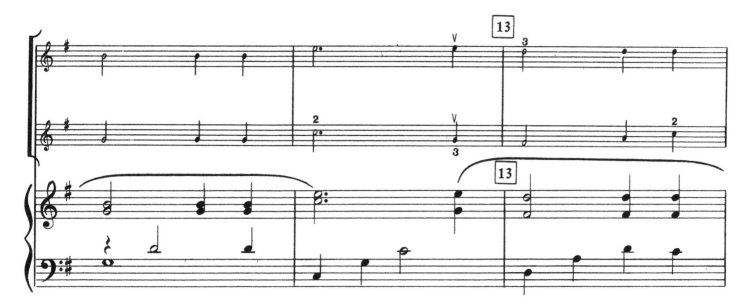

PAT-A-PAN

French Carol

1st Violin

2nd Violin

Piano

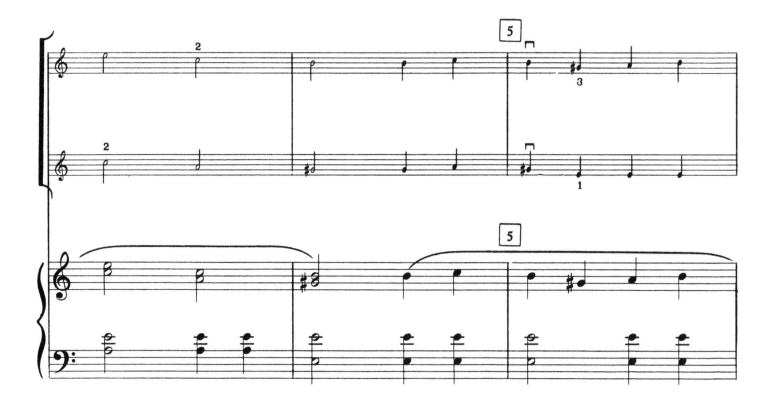

UP ON THE HOUSETOP

Traditional

Violins

Betty N. Barlow

EASIEST VIOLIN DUETS FOR CHRISTMAS

BOOK ONE

CONTENTS

G. SCHIRMER, Inc.

DISTRIBUTED BY

HAL•LEONARD®
CORPORATION

7777 W. BLUEMOUND RD. P.O. BOX 13819 MILWAUKEE, WI 53213

ED. 3208

EASIEST VIOLIN DUETS FOR CHRISTMAS
with Piano Accompaniment

Arrangements by
Betty M. Barlow

JOLLY OLD SAINT NICHOLAS

Traditional

1st Violin
2nd Violin

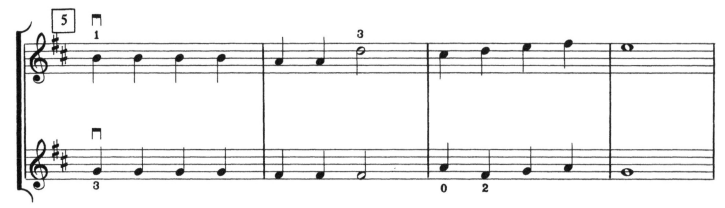

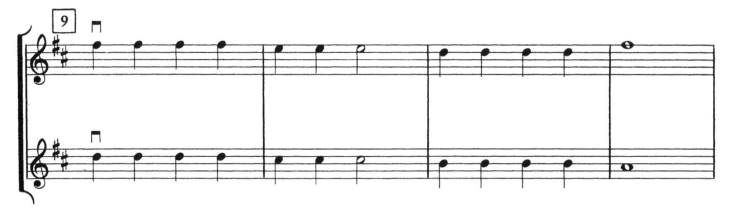

48146c

GOOD KING WENCESLAS

1st Violin

2nd Violin

Traditional

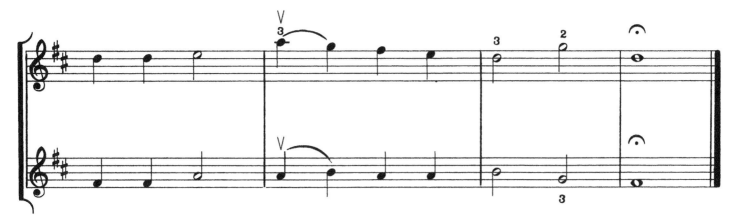

48146

WE THREE KINGS OF ORIENT ARE

John H. Hopkins

1st Violin

2nd Violin

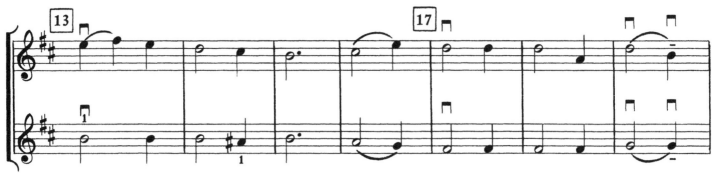

MARY HAD A BABY

Traditional

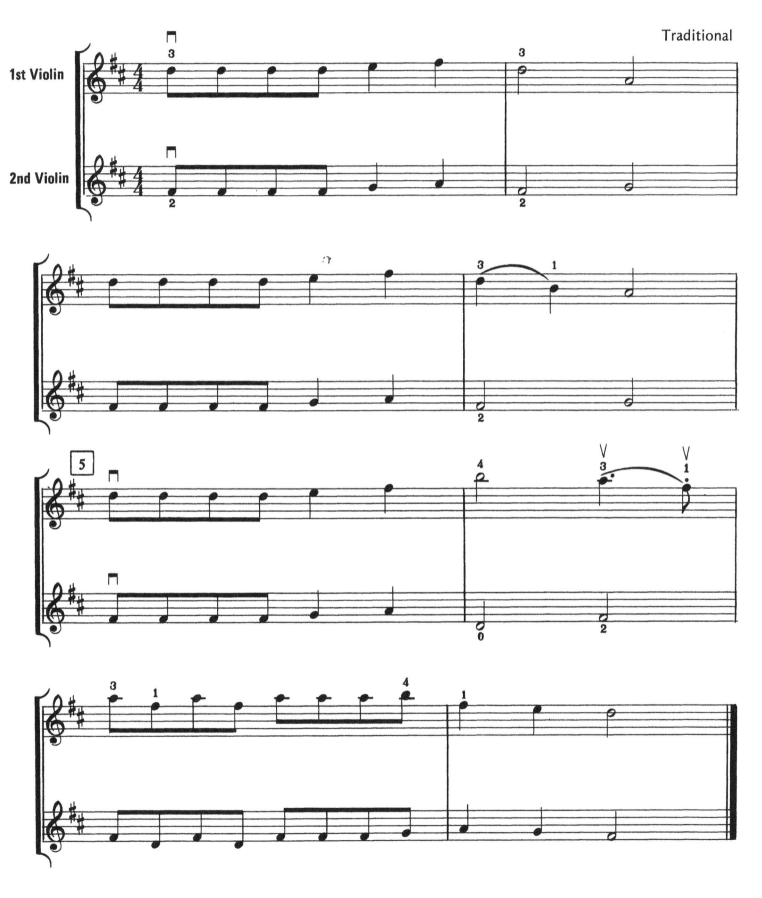

BRING A TORCH, JEANNETTE, ISABELLA

French Carol

1st Violin

2nd Violin

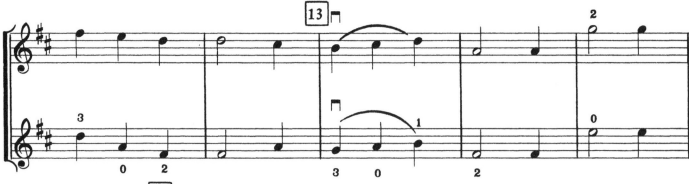

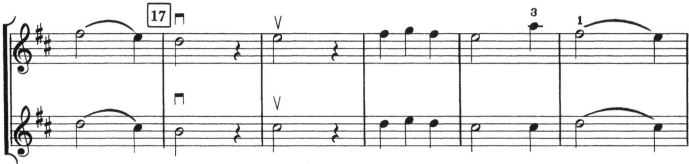

O COME LITTLE CHILDREN

J.A.P. Schulz

PAT-A-PAN

French Carol

1st Violin

2nd Violin

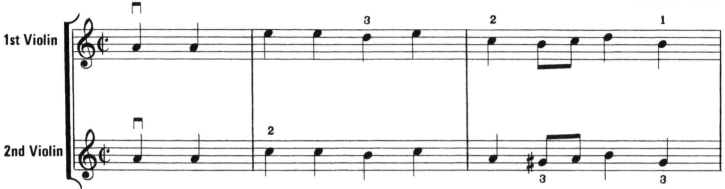

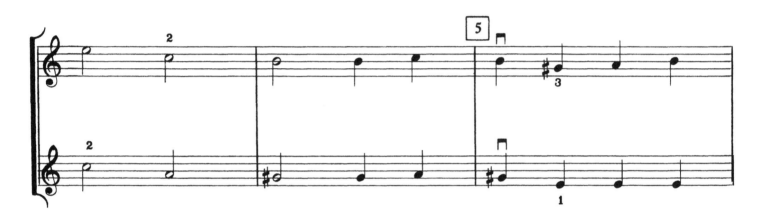

UP ON THE HOUSETOP

Traditional

1st Violin
2nd Violin

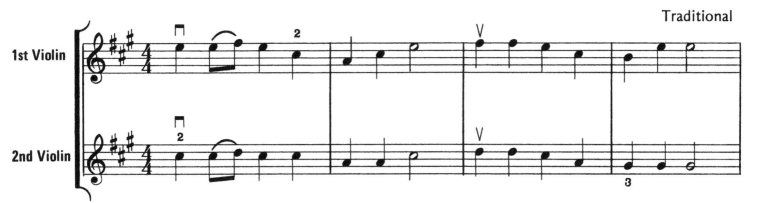

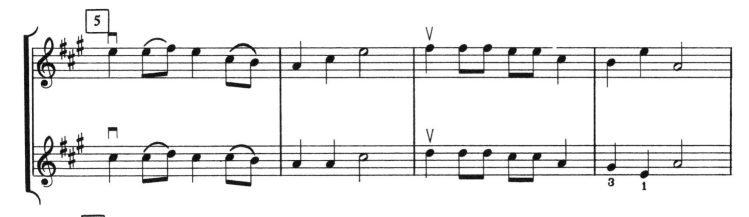

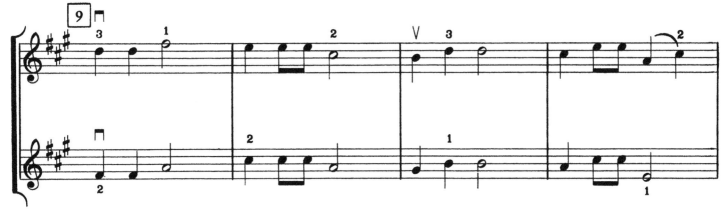

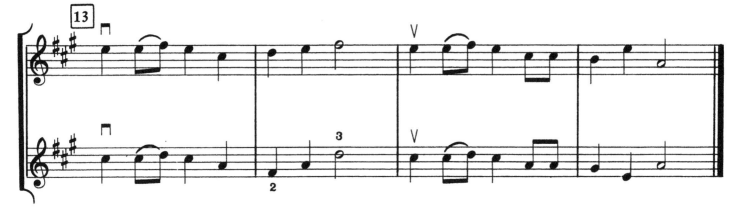

AUSTRIAN CAROL

1st Violin

2nd Violin

WE WISH YOU A MERRY CHRISTMAS

English Carol

1st Violin

2nd Violin

POLISH CAROL

1st Violin

2nd Violin

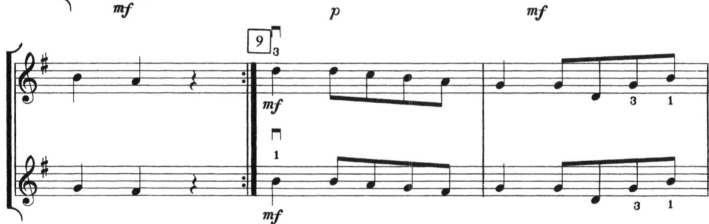

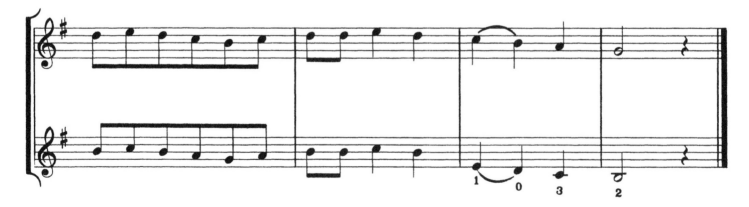

RING, LITTLE BELLS

German Carol

1st Violin

2nd Violin

48146

BORN IS HE, THIS HOLY CHILD

French Carol

1st Violin

2nd Violin

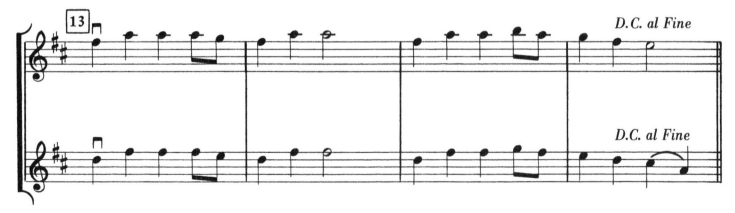

GOD REST YE MERRY, GENTLEMEN

English Carol

1st Violin

2nd Violin

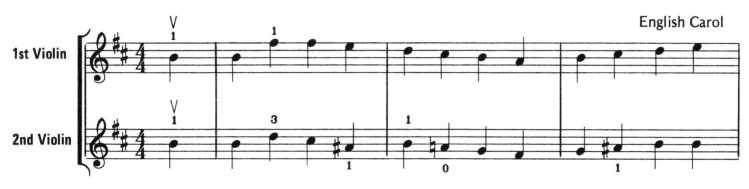

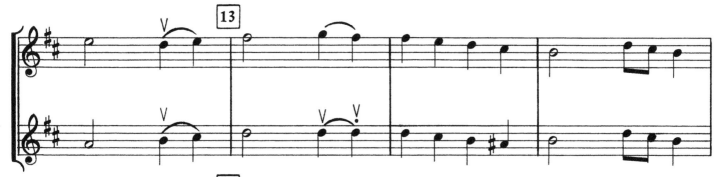

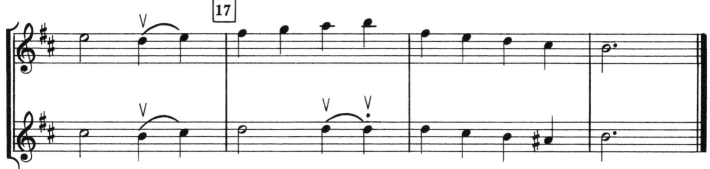

O LITTLE TOWN OF BETHLEHEM

Lewis H. Redner

1st Violin

2nd Violin

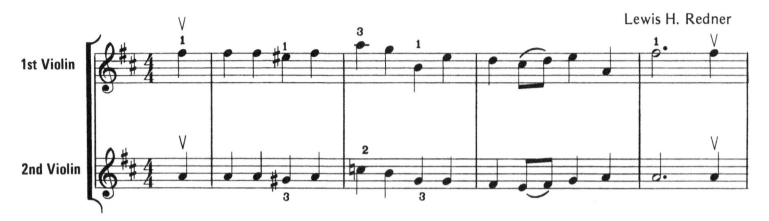

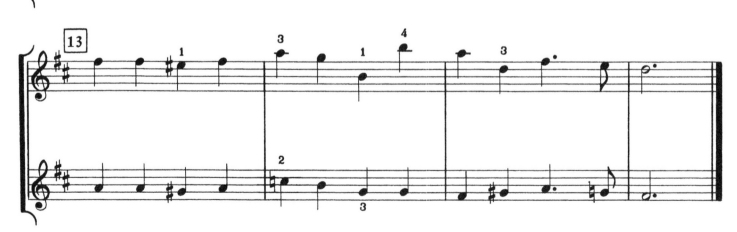

Violins

Betty N. Barlow

EASIEST VIOLIN DUETS FOR CHRISTMAS

BOOK ONE

CONTENTS

G. SCHIRMER, Inc.

DISTRIBUTED BY

HAL•LEONARD®
CORPORATION
7777 W. BLUEMOUND RD. P.O. BOX 13819 MILWAUKEE, WI 53213

ED. 3208

EASIEST VIOLIN DUETS FOR CHRISTMAS
with Piano Accompaniment

Arrangements by
Betty M. Barlow

JOLLY OLD SAINT NICHOLAS

Traditional

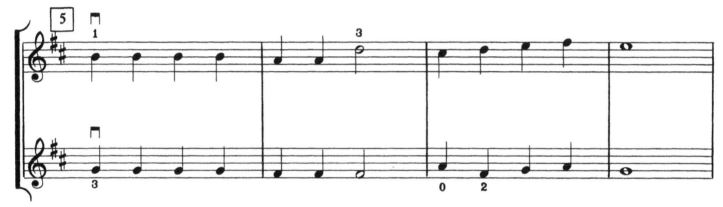

48146c

GOOD KING WENCESLAS

Traditional

1st Violin
2nd Violin

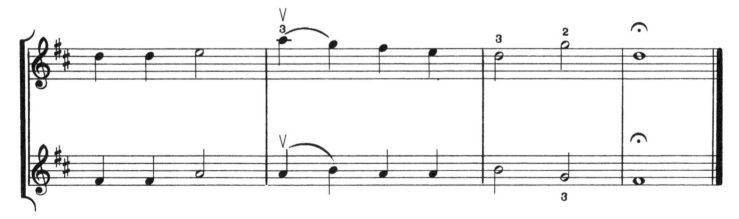

WE THREE KINGS OF ORIENT ARE

John H. Hopkins

1st Violin

2nd Violin

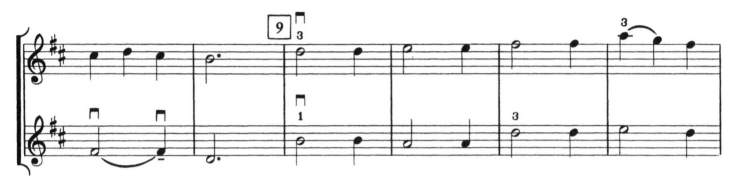

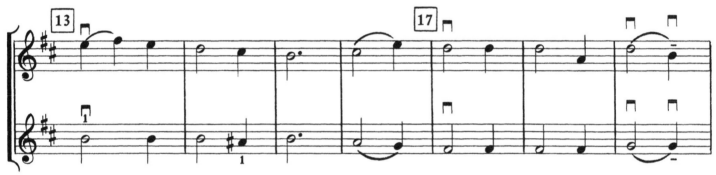

MARY HAD A BABY

Traditional

BRING A TORCH, JEANNETTE, ISABELLA

French Carol

1st Violin

2nd Violin

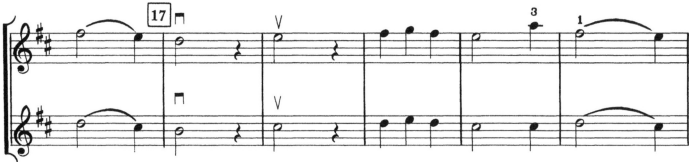

O COME LITTLE CHILDREN

J.A.P. Schulz

1st Violin

2nd Violin

48146

PAT-A-PAN

French Carol

1st Violin

2nd Violin

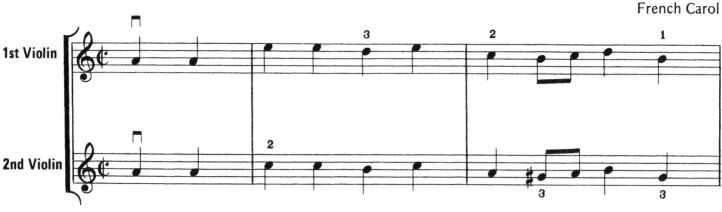

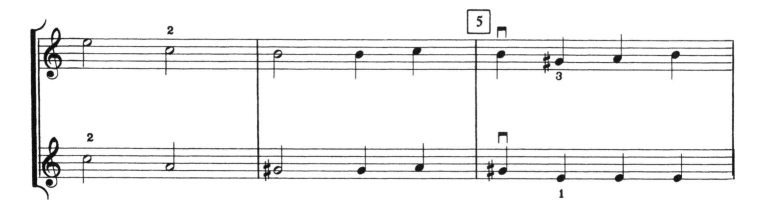

UP ON THE HOUSETOP

Traditional

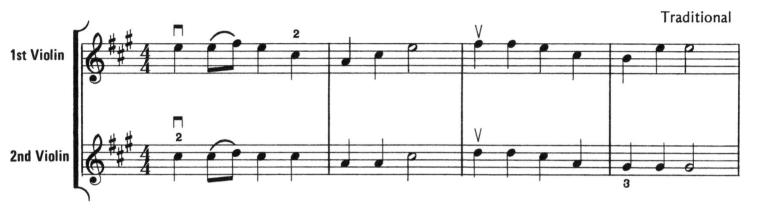

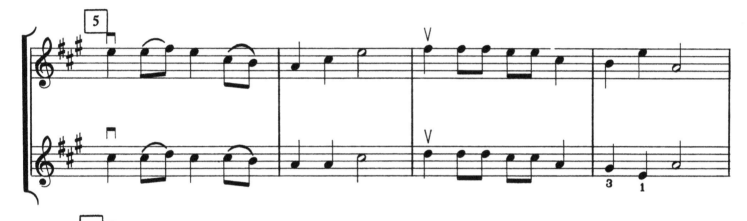

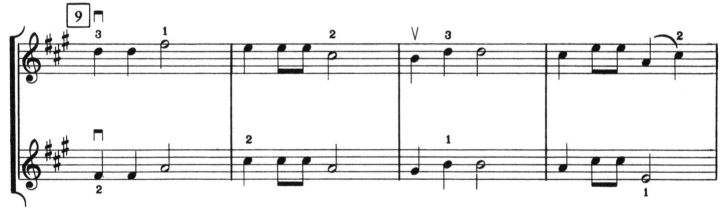

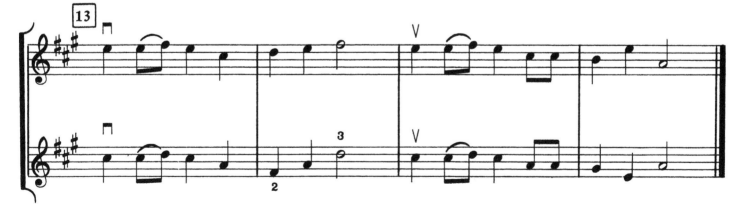

AUSTRIAN CAROL

WE WISH YOU A MERRY CHRISTMAS

English Carol

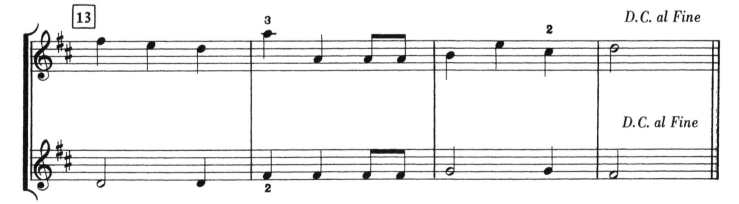

48146

POLISH CAROL

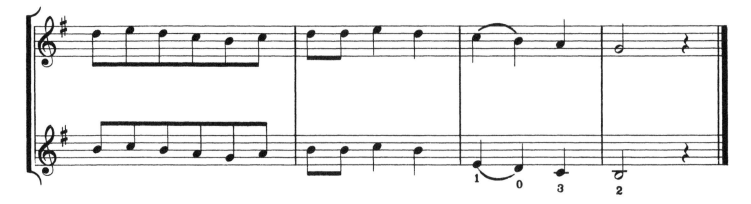

RING, LITTLE BELLS

German Carol

1st Violin

2nd Violin

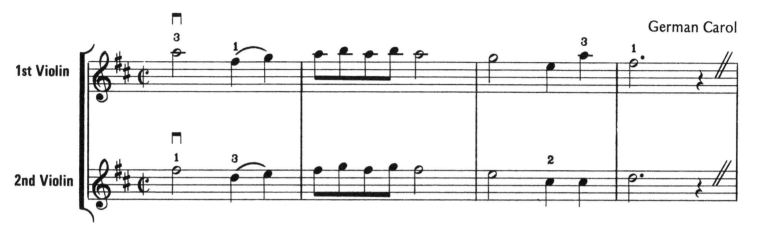

48146

BORN IS HE, THIS HOLY CHILD

French Carol

1st Violin

2nd Violin

GOD REST YE MERRY, GENTLEMEN

English Carol

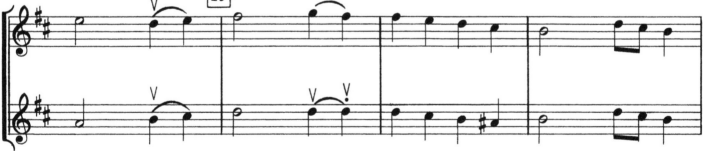

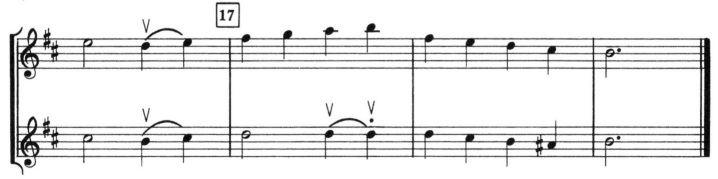

O LITTLE TOWN OF BETHLEHEM

Lewis H. Redner

1st Violin

2nd Violin

AUSTRIAN CAROL

1st Violin

2nd Violin

Piano

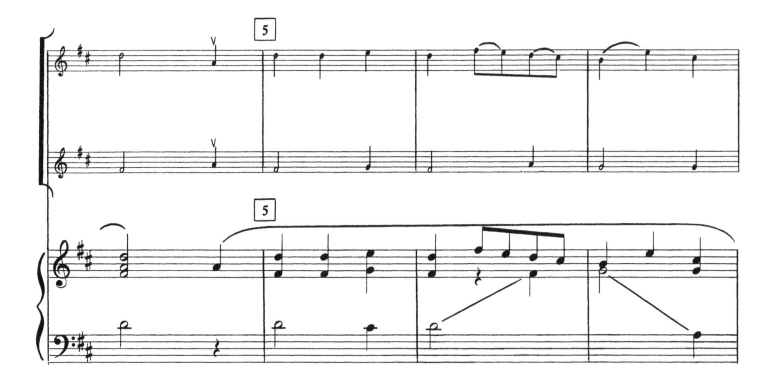

48146

WE WISH YOU A MERRY CHRISTMAS

English Carol

1st Violin

2nd Violin

Piano

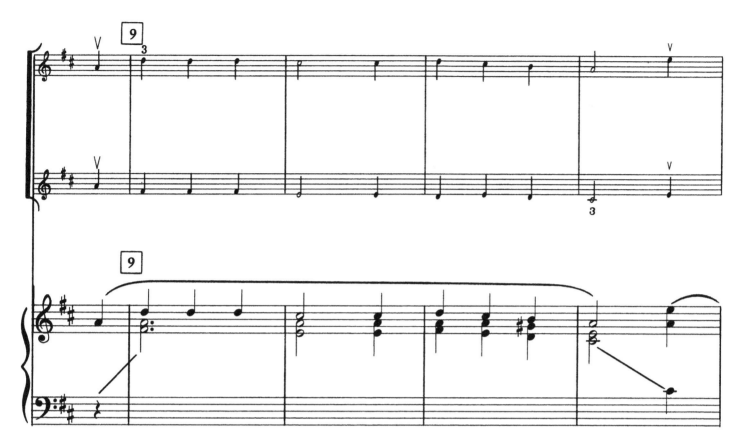

48146

POLISH CAROL

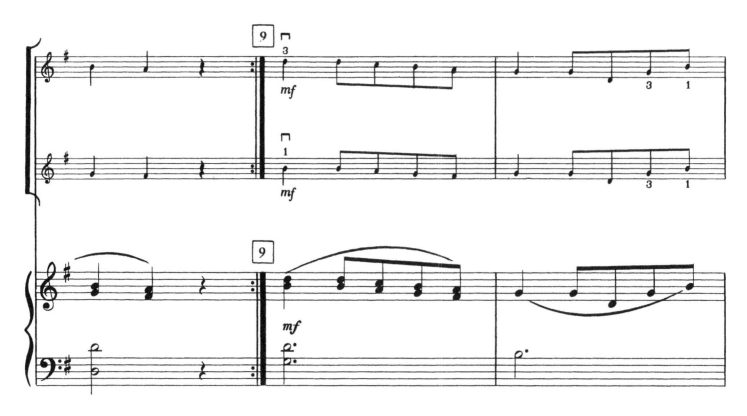

RING, LITTLE BELLS

German Carol

1st Violin

2nd Violin

Piano

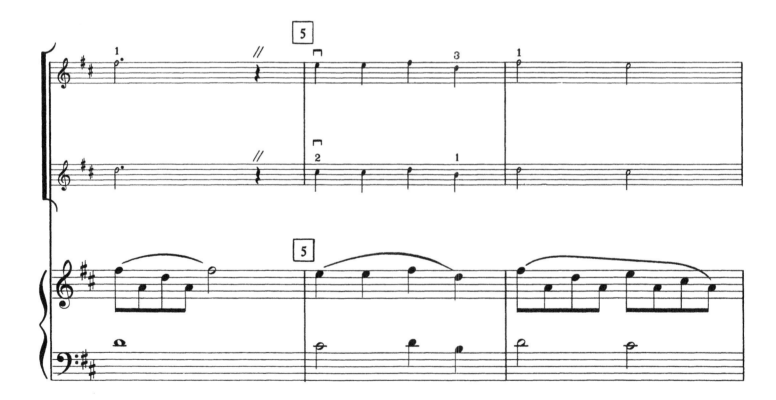

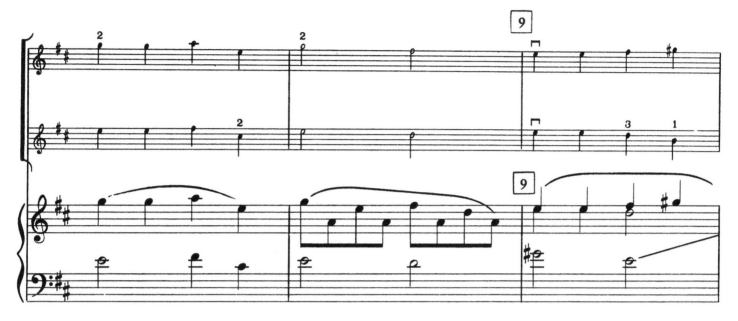

BORN IS HE, THIS HOLY CHILD

French Carol

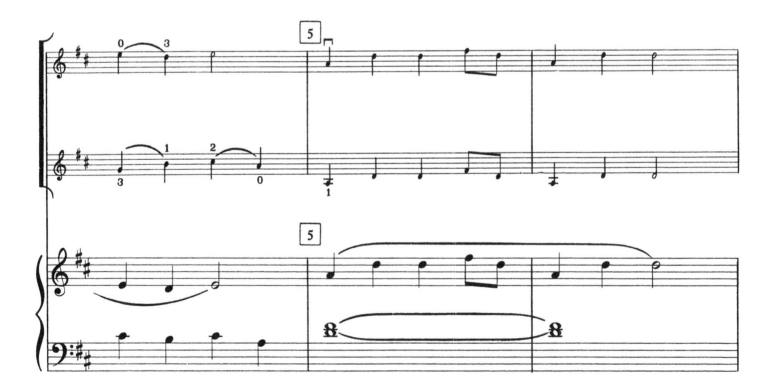

26

48146

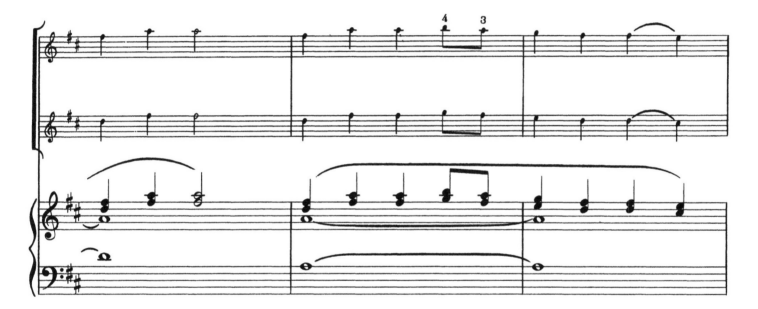

GOD REST YE MERRY, GENTLEMEN

English Carol

1st Violin

2nd Violin

Piano

48146

O LITTLE TOWN OF BETHLEHEM

Lewis H. Redner

48146

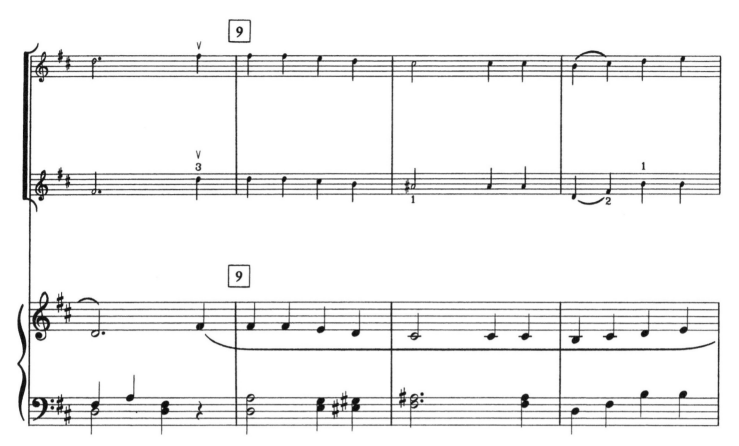

48146